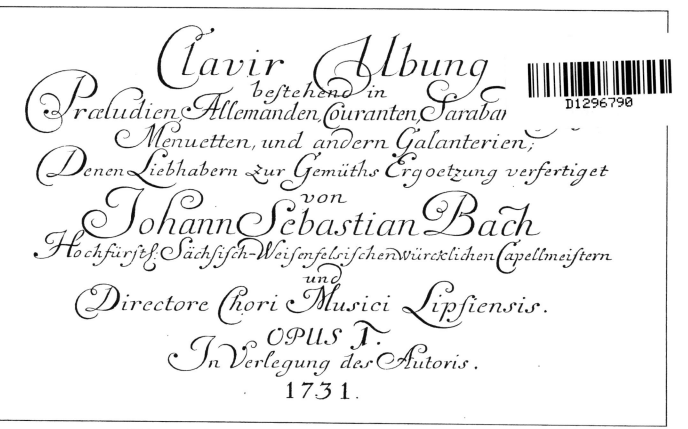

Title page of Bach's own edition of the *Clavierübung*, Part One.
Courtesy of the Library of Congress, Washington, D.C.

ORIGIN

Bach was the author of four volumes entitled *Clavierübung*:

1. *Clavierübung I,* consisting of six *Partitas.*

2. *Clavierübung II,* the *Italian Concerto* and the *Partita in B Minor* (the so-called *French Ouverture).*

3. *Clavierübung III,* consisting of various preludes for organ based on chorales.

4. *Clavierübung IV,* an aria with 30 variations, which became known as the *Goldberg Variations.*

Partita No. 1 in Bb Major is one of the six *Partitas* that make up the first volume of the *Clavierübung.* The title page of the first edition, published by Bach himself and reproduced above is translated as:

Keyboard Training, consisting of Preludes, Allemandes, Courantes, Sarabandes, Gigues, Menuets and other Galanteries, dedicated to Music Lovers for the Pleasure of their Minds, by Johann Sebastian Bach, acting Chapel-master at the Court of Saxe-Weisen-fels, and Director of the Leipzig Musical Choir. Opus 1. Published by the Author. 1731.

The first five of the six *Partitas* comprising this volume had appeared singly between the years 1726 and 1730. In 1731 Bach brought these together with the sixth *Partita* and published them as his Opus 1. J. S. Bach had, of course, composed hundreds of works previous to the *Partitas,* and one of his vocal works, the Mühlhausen *Rathwechsel Cantata* of 1708, had been engraved, but it was the custom of that day to put opus numbers only on published instrumental works.

Some authorities have contended that Bach not only published the *Partitas* himself but that the first edition was engraved on copper plates in the composer's own hand. It seems certain that the engraving was supervised by Bach. Many of his characteristic habits of writing are seen in the engraving, but the shapes of some of the ornaments seem to definitely indicate they were drawn by another hand.

Cover art: Landscape with Roman ruins, *1740*
by Giovanni Antonio Canaletto (1697–1768)
Accademia, Venice, Italy
Cameraphoto/Art Resource, New York

Johann Nicolaus Forkel, who wrote the first biography of J. S. Bach in 1802, gives us the following information about the success of these *Partitas*. His report is based on information he obtained from two of Bach's sons, Wilhelm Friedemann and Carl Philipp Emanuel.

This work made a great sensation in the world of music. Such excellent compositions for the keyboard had never before been seen or heard. Anyone who had learned to play some of these pieces well could make his fortune in the world thereby, and even in our own times a young artist may gain recognition by doing so, they are so brilliant, so well-sounding, so expressive, and they are always new.

Although no autograph of the first *Partita* is known to exist, the composer's edition, if not engraved by the composer himself, was undoubtedly copied from an autograph. In preparing the present edition, five different copies of the composer's edition were consulted:

1. The copy belonging to the Library of Congress. A facsimile of the first *Partita* from this copy is reproduced on pages 7 through 11.

2. The copy from the Hirsch Collection of the British Museum.

3. The copy from the general collection of the British Museum (K 10 a 1).

4. The copy from the Staatsbibliothek (Unter den Linden 8), Berlin, Musikabteilung.

5. The copy from the Riemenschneider Bach Institute at Baldwin-Wallace College, Berea, Ohio.

The following 18th-century manuscripts were also consulted:

1. A copy from the estate of J. N. Forkel, Bach Mus. Ms. P212, which contains only the *Praeludium, Allemande, Corrente* and *Giga.*

2. A copy from the Hartung legacy, Bach Mus. Ms. P215, in the hand of Johann Christoph Ritter.

Microfilms of these two manuscripts were kindly furnished by the Staatsbibliothek (Preussischer Kulturbesitz), Berlin, Musikabteilung.

For an accurate presentation of the text it was necessary to consult several copies of the composer's edition, since it is often impossible to identify certain ornaments, accidentals, etc., that may have been carefully added to the printed copy by another hand. The *Praeludium* of the first *Partita* in the Hirsch copy seems to show a number of refinements in note stems, extensions of leger lines and added ornaments. In the 2nd *Menuet* a schleifer appears in both the Hirsch copy and the copy of the Library of Congress, almost identical in appearance and placement. Problems such as this could be easily resolved if the original plates could be consulted. Unfortunately, they were sold for their copper value during the lifetime of Bach's son, Carl Philipp Emanuel.

BACH'S TABLE OF ORNAMENTS

The following table of ornaments, entitled *Explication unterschiedlicher Zeichen, so gewisse Manieren artig zu spielen, andeuten* (Explanation of various signs, showing how to play certain ornaments properly) is the only such table known to have been prepared by J. S. Bach.

From the *Clavier-Büchlein vor Wilhelm Friedemann Bach*
by Courtesy of the Yale University Music Library

ORNAMENTS IN THE PARTITA

The above table will serve to show the general configuration of most of the ornaments in Bach's first *Partita*. For a thorough discussion of Bach's ornaments, see the foreword of the Alfred Masterwork edition of J. S. Bach's *Inventions and Sinfonias.*

A few remarks about the performance of the trill are in order:

The symbols ⋀ and ⋀⋀ are used interchangeably by Bach and indicate a long or short trill.

All trills begin on the UPPER NOTE.

The number of repercussions in a trill is determined by the tempo of the selection and the time value of the note upon which it occurs. The minimum number of notes in a trill is four.

The trill may come to rest on the principal note but at times may continue for the entire value of the note.

The above rules are confirmed in C. P. E. Bach's *Essay.*

The first *Partita* contains several ornaments not found in the Bach table:

1. THE LONG MORDENT
sometimes called the DOUBLE MORDENT

In Carl Philipp Emanuel Bach's *Essay on the True Art of Playing Keyboard Instruments,* he gives the following execution for the long and short mordents.

THE LONG MORDENT

written: played: or:

THE SHORT MORDENT

written: played:

The addition of the sharp sign before the F in the realization of the short mordent is explained by the following quotation from C. P. E. Bach's *Essay:*

> *In the matter of accidentals this ornament [the mordent] adjusts itself to circumstances in the same manner as the trill [that is, it uses the tones of the prevailing key]. Its brilliance is often increased by raising the lower tone.*

Mordents are always played ON THE BEAT.

---

2. THE APPOGGIATURA
indicated by a small note ♪

Bach's table of ornaments shows appoggiaturas indicated by the sign ᴎ.

The appoggiatura is always played ON THE BEAT. It takes half the value of the following note, except when the following note is dotted.

It then usually takes two thirds of the value of this note.

The modern "grace note" ♪ was not used by Bach, and editions containing such an ornament are incorrect.

---

3. THE SCHLEIFER ⌒

This ornament is called the "slide." This type of schleifer adds the two lower neighboring tones before the principal note, which follows the sign.

The ornament is played ON THE BEAT, and the values of the added notes are subtracted from the principal note. It is always played rapidly.

The only example of a schleifer in the first *Partita* is found in the 2nd *Menuet,* page 28, in measure 14. The ornament is found in the Hirsch copy and in the copy of the Library of Congress, very probably added by hand.

written: played:

EARLY TRADITIONS IN MUSIC WRITING

Before studying the composer's edition, the student should be alerted to certain 18th-century practices in music writing which are no longer observed. The key signature, for example, seems to show three rather than two flats. This is because the E♭ is duplicated in the treble (upper space and lower line) and the B♭ is duplicated in the bass at the extremes of the staff.

It should also be noted that an accidental generally affected only the note immediately following the sign. Good examples of this practice are found in measure 5 of the *Allemande* (page 8).

In the newly engraved text of the *Partita* in this edition, beginning on page 12, the modern rules regarding accidentals are observed.

The signs at the ends of some of the staffs (for example, at the end of the first line of the *Praeludium,* on page 7) are neither notes nor ornaments, although they resemble the ornament known as the *schleifer.* These signs, called *directs,* simply show at the end of the line the notes that are to begin the following line.

Signs indicating notes that
begin the next line of music.

Many composers of the 18th century continued the early practice of writing long, unbroken leger lines that extended as far as they were useful in any particular passage. Several examples of this may be found in the composer's edition. See the last three measures of the *Praeludium,* (page 7).

NOTE STEMS

The directions of note stems in the composer's edition of the *Partita* make a particularly interesting study. These stem directions are followed closely in the manuscript copies mentioned in our sources (page 2). In his book, *Musical Autographs* (Dover Publications, N.Y., 1965), Emanuel Winternitz calls attention to the fact that Carl Philipp Emanuel Bach wrote certain groups of notes in one of his autographs as follows:

Dr. Winternitz observes that this particular grouping of the notes clarifies the aim of the composer.

In the *Clavierübung,* the note stems often seem to clarify the construction of the music and to define certain note groupings and phrases. In measures 13-15 of the *Corrente,* (page 9), the directions of the note stems seem to outline the most logical phrasing of the right hand part.

suggests the following:

The note stems in the upper staff at the very beginning of the same movement are also worthy of attention. If they do not indicate phrasing, they certainly clarify the structure by clearly defining the motive upon which the movement is constructed.

indicates the following construction:

The note stems of the left hand part in measure 4 of the same movement are also interesting. In measure 5 the left hand plays the motive of the opening measures, and the stem directions are consistent with those used previously in the upper staff.

Bach also used stem directions to show which hand should be used to play certain notes. This cannot be more clearly illustrated than in the *Giga,* (page 11).

Before leaving this topic it is well to consider the fact that some of the stem directions may result simply from Bach's routine procedures in writing. It is very likely that some of the noteheads and stems were drawn, for example, as follows, without regard to the fact that beams were to be added later:

When the beams were added, this was the result:

The stem directions of measure 28 of the 1st *Menuet,* (page 10) cannot be explained on any musical basis and can only be the result of the writing practice just mentioned.

It is also true that note stem patterns that may be construed to reveal articulation and/or construction of the music are not always followed through consistently in the course of the movement. This fact would not make the whole premise invalid, however, since on the few occasions that Bach wrote slurs, he almost invariably wrote them over a few notes or for a few measures and then discontinued them because it was obvious that similar patterns should be played as previously indicated.

It is important, nevertheless, to weigh such factors in forming an opinion as to the intention of the composer to use stem directions to indicate articulation or anything special in a particular passage.

In the newly engraved edition in this book, we have retained stem directions that may have meaning with respect to performance of the work, except in those cases where modern engraving techniques would make such passages more difficult to read.

THE VARIABLE DOT

In baroque notation, the value of the dot placed after a note was variable. Although it was generally performed according to our modern rules, it was lengthened or shortened in certain circumstances.

Values of dots were prolonged in certain passages of slow movements, according to Leopold Mozart, "to prevent the performance from sounding too lethargic." This is confirmed in C. P. E. Bach's *Essay* and by other writers of the period.

This practice, called "overdotting," may be applied effectively in the opening measures of the *Sarabande,* (page 22) and in similar passages.

written:

played:

(continued on page 32)

Partita No. 1 in B♭ Major from Bach's own edition of the *Clavierübung, Part One.*
Courtesy of the Library of Congress, Washington, D.C.
(Measure numbers have been added for reference purposes.)

Allemande.

Sarabande.

Menuets.

Menuetz.

10

PARTITA 1

Praeludium

Andante M.M. ♪ = 84-96

(a) Ornaments in light print are present in the Hirsch copy in the British Museum and appear to have been added on the plates. See the discussion on page 2. In any case, these ornaments are obviously required and should be played.

Allemande

Allegro moderato M.M. ♩ = 88-100

(a) In the composer's edition the natural sign appears after the E rather than before it. It is correctly placed in the Hartung manuscript (P215).

(b) Stem directions in this measure are the editor's and are used only to clarify which notes are to be taken by right and left hands.

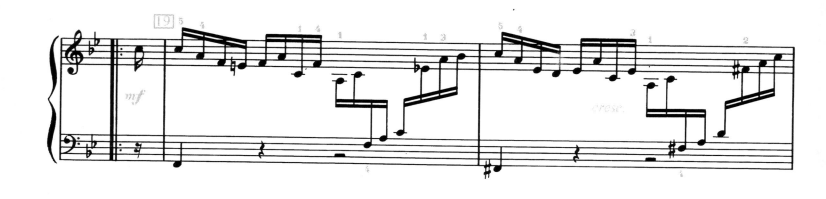

ⓒ In the composer's edition the trill is on the preceding note (F). It is similarly placed in the Forkel manuscript (P212). In the Hartung manuscript (P215) it is missing completely. Our text is based on the presumption that this measure should agree with measure 12.

ⓓ The D is from the composer's edition. The Forkel and Hartung manuscripts have C.

Corrente

ⓐ Each sixteenth note is played simultaneously with the last eighth note of the triplet, in accordance with the tradition of the period. See the discussion, "The Variable Dot," beginning on page 6.

ⓑ The trills may be played with more repercussions, depending on the tempo.

ⓒ The natural sign is missing in the composer's edition but is present in the Hartung manuscript (P215).

19

(d) The composer's edition has F instead of G. In the copy of the Staatsbibliothek it is corrected to a G. The Forkel manuscript (P212) also has G. The G seems best, since it avoids the effect of the doubled seventh. The parallel situation two measures later indicates that the G is correct.

(e) The natural sign before the first E is missing in the composer's edition but is present in the Hartung manuscript (P215).

(f) In the composer's edition the trill is over the D♮. In the Forkel manuscript it is definitely over the E♭. There is no ornament here in the Hartung manuscript.

Sarabande

Un poco lento   M.M. ♪ = 76-84

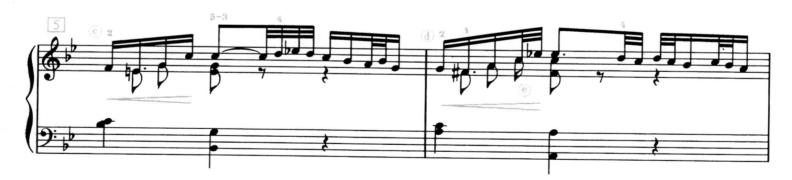

(a) All chords in this movement may be arpeggiated, from the lowest note to the highest, or vice versa.

(b) The ties in light print are found only in the Hartung manuscript (P215).

(c) The Hartung manuscript has

(d) The Hartung manuscript has

(e) In the composer's edition the downstem has only one flag, but it can only be a sixteenth note.

(f) In some editions the rhythm is "corrected":

It seems more likely that the following is correct:

(g) Some editions have . The Hartung manuscript has

The following may be more correct:

(h) The downstems are from the composer's edition. Most modern editions omit the downstem on the A.

(i) The natural sign is missing in the composer's edition and in the Hartung manuscript. This is undoubtedly an oversight.

ⓙ Some modern editions have applied the same "correction" here as at ⓕ.

Menuet 1

ⓐ The quarter notes in the left hand of the 1st *Menuet* are traditionally played detached, while the right hand notes are played legato.

ⓑ The Hartung manuscript (P215) has F instead of E♭.

Menuet 2

(a) For the origin of the schleifer see the discussion on page 4. This is certainly a proper application of this ornament, even though it is not found in the original engraving.

(b) The Hartung manuscript (P215) has A instead of B♭.

Giga

(a) Bach used the extra long stems on the quarter notes in the lower staff to indicate that these notes are to be played with the right hand and the eighth-note triplets with the left. This is somewhat difficult on the modern piano, particularly in certain measures (for example, measure 28). The modern practice of playing the quarter notes with the left hand and the triplets with the right probably originated with the Czerny edition. The movement contains no fingering problems, and we have left it unfingered to avoid imposing either of the two alternatives on the individual.

Ⓑ Here the Hartung manuscript (P 215) has the following:

THE VARIABLE DOT (continued from page 6)

Dotted eighths and sixteenths were sometimes "underdotted" when appearing against triplet rhythm. C. P. E. Bach gives the following example:

In modern notation this example could be written:

In his book, *The Interpretation of the Music of the 17th and 18th Centuries* (Oxford University Press, London, 1915), Arnold Dolmetsch chose the *Corrente* from this work as an example of the application of this practice.

written:

played:

TITLES OF MOVEMENTS PROVIDE CLUES TO STYLE

Intensifications of dotted rhythms are generally more applicable to French music than to Italian music. In Italian music dotted rhythms are usually adapted to fit the dominant rhythm of the movement. The first *Partita* contains two movements with Italian titles, the *Corrente*, and the *Giga*. Most editions, even including the Bach-Gesellschaft, have changed these titles to the French *Courante* and *Gigue*.

Philipp Spitta, in his monumental work, *Johann Sebastian Bach* (1879), now reprinted by Dover Publications, discusses the importance of the retention of the original titles of the movements of Bach's suites, since they provide clues to their interpretation.

The Italian *corrente*, in $\frac{3}{4}$ or $\frac{3}{8}$ time and played in a smooth, rapid style, differs from the more impassioned yet solid and grave French *courante*, which is often in $\frac{3}{2}$ time. The dots are not lengthened in the Italian *corrente*, and in the case of the *Corrente* in this *Partita*, they are assimilated into the basic rhythm to preserve the fluidity of the movement.

The Italian *giga*, always in triple meter, is more homophonic in structure than the French *gigue*, which is often in $\frac{6}{8}$ or in *alla breve* time. The last movement of this *Partita* certainly answers all the requirements for the Italian *giga*, both in style and technique. The crossing of the hands, characteristic of the harpsichord music of Domenico Scarlatti, was a device that enjoyed great popularity at the time the *Partitas* were published.

It seems clear that Bach used the Italian titles *Corrente* and *Giga* with a purpose. The *Sarabande*, with its French title, invites performance in the French manner.

It is only from Bach's autographs and from his own editions that these titles may be learned. Even the standard reference work, the Schmieder *Bach-Werke-Verzeichnis*, has corrupted the titles. In that work there is no distinction between Bach's *Correntes* and *Courantes*. *Menuets* and *Minuettas* are called *Menuetts*. *Gavottas* and *Gavottes* are all *Gavottes*, etc. Thurston Dart has summarized our convictions in his excellent book, *The Interpretation of Music* (Harper & Row, New York, 1954), when he calls attention to the fact that the words *allemande, courante, sarabande, menuet* and *gigue* normally imply the French style. *Allemanda, coranto* or *corrente, sarabanda, minuetta* and *giga* imply the Italian style. Thus it is important that Bach's original titles be carefully preserved.

TOUCH AND ARTICULATION

In his biography of J. S. Bach, Forkel describes the touch Bach cultivated in his students as being such that "the tones are neither disjoined from each other nor blended together." To this he adds, "the touch is, therefore, as C. Ph. Emanuel Bach says, neither too long nor too short, but just what it ought to be." He mentioned that Bach played with curved fingers, with the tips perpendicular to the keys, and with a very quiet hand and arm. The result, he said, was "the highest degree of clearness in the expression of individual notes."

These comments, taken from information given to Forkel by Bach's sons, can be applied to Bach's music only in a general way. Bach certainly stressed legato playing and emphasized the importance of the cantabile style in the foreword to the *INVENTIONS & SINFONIAS.* C. P. E. Bach points out that the legato style is especially appropriate in slow music and the detached style in faster movements.

EDITORIAL SUGGESTIONS

The composer's edition of the first *Partita* contains no tempo or dynamic indications and no slurs. The indications in light print have been added by the editor and may be observed according to the discretion of the individual.

ACKNOWLEDGEMENTS

I would like to express my appreciation to Judith Simon Linder for her valuable assistance in the research necessary for the realization of this edition, and for her help in preparing the manuscript.

I also wish to thank Iris and Morton Manus for their help with the final layout, for supervising the engraving and printing, and for making many valuable suggestions.

I am also indebted to William Lichtenwanger, head of the Music Division, Reference Department, Library of Congress, for giving so warmly and generously of his time to help with this project.